BACK OR FRONT LOOP ONLY

Work only in loop(s) indicated by arrow *(Fig. 1)*.

Fig. 1

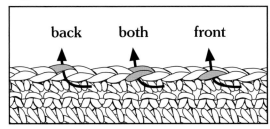

FREE LOOPS

After working in Back or Front Loops Only on a row or round, there will be a ridge of unused loops. These are called the free loops. Later, when instructed to work in the free loops of the same row or round, work in these loops *(Fig. 2a)*.

When instructed to work in free loops of a chain, work in loop indicated by arrow *(Fig. 2b)*.

Fig. 2a   **Fig. 2b**

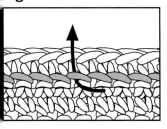
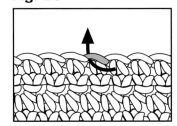

POST STITCH

Work around post of stitch indicated, inserting hook in direction of arrow *(Fig. 3)*.

Fig. 3

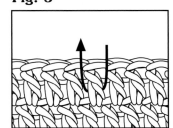

CHANGING

Work the last stitch to
hook new yarn *(Fig.*
on hook. Cut old yar

Fig. 4a   **Fig. 4b**

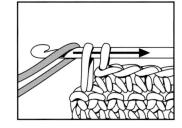
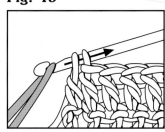

EMBROIDERY
STRAIGHT STITCH

Straight Stitch is just what the name implies, a single, straight stitch. Come up at 1 and go down at 2 *(Fig. 5)*.

Fig. 5

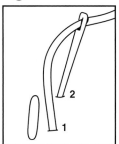

LAZY DAISY STITCH

Make all loops equal in length. Bring needle up at 1 and make a counterclockwise loop with the yarn. Go down at 1 and come up at 2, keeping the yarn below the point of the needle *(Fig. 6)*. Secure loop by bringing yarn over loop and down at 3.

Fig. 6

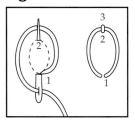

Production Team: Writer - Susan Ackerman Carter; Technical Editor - Linda Luder; Editorial Writer - Suzie Puckett; Artist - Lora Puls; and Photo Stylist - Janna Laughlin.

Dishcloths made and instructions tested by Janet Akins, Belinda Baxter, Katie Galucki, Dale Potter, and Cathy Wyatt.

First Prize

Joan E. Reeves of Texas, our First-Prize winner, has been crocheting since she was a little girl. She started modifying patterns and designing her own about six years ago. "I really enjoy making things for the kitchen," she says. A wife, mother, and grandmother, Joan also likes crocheting baby items and toys. "I usually don't have a pattern in mind when I start; it just sort of develops as I go along," she explains. In Joan's Sunshine Daisy dishcloth, pretty crocheted petals open out from a plastic scrubber center to make cleanup a breeze.

Joan E. Reeves

SUNSHINE DAISY

Finished Size: 11" from point to point

MATERIALS
100% Cotton Worsted Weight Yarn:
   White - 1³/₄ ounces, (50 grams, 95 yards)
   Green - 16 yards
Crochet hook, size F (3.75 mm) **or** size needed for gauge
3¹/₂" diameter Plastic mesh scouring pad

GAUGE: 9 hdc = 2"

STITCH GUIDE

BEGINNING DECREASE (uses first 2 hdc)
YO, insert hook in first hdc, YO and pull up a loop, YO, insert hook in next hdc, YO and pull up a loop, YO and draw through all 5 loops on hook **(counts as first hdc)**.

DECREASE (uses next 2 hdc)
★ YO, insert hook in **next** hdc, YO and pull up a loop; repeat from ★ once **more**, YO and draw through all 5 loops on hook **(counts as one hdc)**.

CENTER
With knotted ends of pad at center and working through two layers of mesh at outer edge of pad, join White with sc *(see Joining With Sc, page 1)*; work 34 sc evenly spaced around; join with slip st to first sc, do **not** finish off: 35 sc.

FIRST PETAL
Row 1 (Right side)**:** Ch 1, skip first sc, hdc in next 5 sc, leave remaining sc unworked: 5 hdc.

Note: Loop a short piece of yarn around any stitch to mark Row 1 as **right** side.

Rows 2-5: Ch 1, turn; 2 hdc in first hdc, hdc in each hdc across to last hdc, 2 hdc in last hdc: 13 hdc.

Row 6: Ch 1, turn; hdc in first hdc and in each hdc across.

Rows 7-11: Ch 1, turn; work beginning decrease, hdc in each hdc across to last 2 hdc, decrease: 3 hdc.

Row 12: Ch 1, turn; skip first hdc, decrease; finish off: one hdc.

NEXT 5 PETALS
Row 1: With **right** side facing, join White with slip st in same st as last hdc worked on Row 1 of previous Petal; ch 1, hdc in next 5 sc, leave remaining sc unworked: 5 hdc.

Rows 2-12: Work same as First Petal: one hdc.

LAST PETAL
Row 1: With **right** side facing, join White with slip st in same st as last hdc worked on Row 1 of previous Petal; ch 1, hdc in next 4 sc and in same st as joining slip st on Center: 5 hdc.

Rows 2-12: Work same as First Petal; at end of Row 12, do **not** finish off: one hdc.

EDGING
Ch 1, turn; 3 sc in same st, ★ † working in end of rows, sc in first 2 rows, 2 sc in next row, (sc in next 2 rows, 2 sc in next row) across, working between first hdc of Row 1 of same Petal and slip st on Row 1 of next Petal, sc in same st on Center; working in end of rows, 2 sc in first row, sc in next 2 rows, 2 sc in next row, holding next Petal and previous Petal with **wrong** sides together, matching rows, and working through **both** thicknesses, (sc in next row and in corresponding sc on previous Petal) twice, place marker in last sc worked into on previous Petal for st placement, (2 sc in next row, sc in next 2 rows) twice †, 3 sc in hdc at tip of Petal; repeat from ★ 5 times **more**, then repeat from † to † once; join with slip st to first sc, finish off.

LEAF
Row 1: With **right** side facing, join Green with sc in any marked sc; skip joining sc on next Petal, sc in next 4 sc: 5 sc.

Row 2: Ch 1, turn; sc in each sc across, skip next sc on Edging, sc in next sc: 6 sc.

Row 3: Ch 1, turn; sc in each sc across.

Row 4: Ch 1, turn; sc in each sc across, skip next sc on Edging, slip st in next sc.

Row 5: Turn; sc in each sc across; finish off.

Repeat for remaining 6 Leaves.

Second Prize
Hazel Jones

Hazel Jones of Minnesota, our Second-Prize winner, had never entered a design contest before this one, but her divine design caught our eye. The popularity and timeless charm of cherubs was the inspiration behind her Faucet Angel dishcloth. "I enjoy crochet because of the challenge of figuring out the patterns," she shares. In addition to crocheting and working as an engineering assistant for her local telephone company, Hazel enjoys music, downhill skiing, swimming, and various arts and crafts.

FAUCET ANGEL

Finished Size: 10"w x 12"h

MATERIALS
100% Cotton Worsted Weight Yarn:
  $2^1/_4$ ounces, (65 grams, 120 yards)
Crochet hook, size F (3.75 mm) **or** size needed
  for gauge
2" Plastic ring

GAUGE: In pattern, (dc, ch 1) 9 times = 4"

HEAD
Rnd 1 (Right side): Join yarn with sc around plastic ring *(see Joining With Sc, page 1)*; 37 sc around ring; join with slip st to first sc, do **not** finish off: 38 sc.

LEFT WING
Row 1: Ch 21, dc in sixth ch from hook, ★ ch 1, skip next ch, dc in next ch; repeat from ★ across to last 3 chs, ch 3, skip last 3 chs, slip st in same st as joining on Head: 7 dc.

Row 2: Ch 3, turn; (dc in next dc, ch 1) 7 times, skip next ch, dc in next ch: 8 dc.

Row 3: Ch 4 (**counts as first dc plus ch 1, now and throughout**), turn; dc in next dc, (ch 1, dc in next dc) 6 times, ch 3, slip st in next sc on Head.

Row 4: Ch 3, turn; dc in next dc, (ch 1, dc in next dc) across.

Row 5: Ch 4, turn; dc in next dc, (ch 1, dc in next dc) 6 times, ch 3, slip st in next 2 sc on Head.

Rows 6-8: Repeat Rows 4 and 5 once, then repeat Row 4 once **more**.

Row 9: Ch 4, turn; dc in next dc, (ch 1, dc in next dc) 6 times, ch 3, slip st in next sc on Head.

Row 10: Ch 3, turn; dc in next dc, (ch 1, dc in next dc) across; do **not** finish off.

DRESS
Row 1: Ch 25, dc in sixth ch from hook, ch 1, skip next ch, ★ dc in next ch, ch 1, skip next ch; repeat from ★ 8 times **more**, dc in next dc, (ch 1, dc in next dc) 7 times, ch 3, slip st in next 2 sc on Head: 18 dc.

Row 2: Ch 3, turn; 2 dc in each dc across to last sp, skip next ch, dc in next ch: 37 dc.

Row 3: Ch 4, turn; skip next dc, dc in next dc, ★ ch 1, skip next dc, dc in next dc; repeat from ★ across, ch 3, slip st in next 2 sc on Head: 19 dc.

Row 4: Ch 3, turn; 2 dc in each dc across to last dc, dc in last dc: 37 dc.

Row 5: Ch 4, turn; skip next dc, dc in next dc, ★ ch 1, skip next dc, dc in next dc; repeat from ★ across, ch 3, slip st in next sc on Head: 19 dc.

Row 6: Ch 3, turn; 2 dc in each dc across to last dc, dc in last dc: 37 dc.

Row 7: Ch 4, turn; skip next dc, dc in next dc, ★ ch 1, skip next dc, dc in next dc; repeat from ★ across, ch 3, slip st in next 2 sc on Head: 19 dc.

Row 8: Ch 3, turn; 2 dc in each dc across to last dc, dc in last dc: 37 dc.

Rows 9-19: Repeat Rows 3-8 once, then repeat Rows 3-7 once **more**; at end of Row 19, do **not** finish off.

RIGHT WING
Row 1: Ch 3, turn; dc in next dc, (ch 1, dc in next dc) 7 times, leave remaining 11 dc unworked: 8 dc.

Row 2: Ch 4, turn; dc in next dc, (ch 1, dc in next dc) across, ch 3, slip st in next sc on Head.

Row 3: Ch 3, turn; dc in next dc, (ch 1, dc in next dc) across.

Row 4: Ch 4, turn; dc in next dc, (ch 1, dc in next dc) across, ch 3, slip st in next 2 sc on Head.

Row 5: Ch 3, turn; dc in next dc, (ch 1, dc in next dc) across.

Row 6: Ch 4, turn; dc in next dc, (ch 1, dc in next dc) across, ch 3, slip st in next sc on Head.

Rows 7-10: Repeat Rows 5 and 6 twice; at end of Row 10, do **not** finish off.

Continued on page 5.

EDGING

Working in unworked sc on Head, sc in next sc, (ch 5, sc in next sc) 7 times; working in free loops *(Fig. 2b, page 2)* and in sps across beginning ch of Left Wing, 3 sc in first sp, sc in next ch, (sc in next sp and in next ch) 7 times; † working in end of rows, 5 dc in top of Row 1, sc in top of next row, (5 dc in top of next row, sc in top of next row) 4 times †; working in free loops and in sps across beginning ch of Dress, (sc in next sp and in next ch) across to last sp, 4 sc in last sp; working in end of rows, 3 sc in next row, (2 sc in next row, 3 sc in next row) 8 times, 4 sc in next sp; working in sts and sps across Row 19 of Dress, sc in next dc, (sc in next sp and in next dc) 10 times, repeat from † to † once; working in sts and sps across Row 10 of Right Wing, (sc in next sp and in next dc) 7 times, 3 sc in next sp; join with slip st to next sc, finish off.

Third Prize
Joyce L. Rodriguez

Joyce L. Rodriguez of California, our Third-Prize winner, has rediscovered the pleasure of crochet. Joyce was 13 when her grandmother taught her to crochet. She says, however, "I didn't get back to it until I retired a few years ago." She has taught three of her grandchildren the basics of crochet in hopes that they, too, will "get back to it" when they're ready. "Now they're teaching me to use the computer. Crocheting is a lot easier!" Joyce laughs. She designed Diamonds for Christmas to feel more like a traditional dishcloth with a texture that's good for scrubbing.

DIAMONDS FOR CHRISTMAS

Finished Size: $10^1/4$"w x $9^1/4$"h

MATERIALS
Bedspread Weight Cotton Thread (size 10):
Variegated - 154 yards
White - 66 yards
Green - 60 yards
Steel crochet hook, size 3 (2.10 mm) **or** size needed for gauge

GAUGE: In pattern, (dc, ch 2) 10 times and 11 rows = 4"

FOUNDATION

With White, ch 80.

Row 1 (Right side)**:** Dc in eighth ch from hook, ★ ch 2, skip next 2 chs, dc in next ch; repeat from ★ across: 25 dc.

Note: Loop a short piece of thread around any stitch to mark Row 1 as **right** side.

Row 2: Ch 5 **(counts as first dc plus ch 2, now and throughout)**, turn; (dc in next dc, ch 2) across, skip next 2 chs, dc in next ch: 26 dc.

Rows 3-12: Ch 5, turn; dc in next dc, (ch 2, dc in next dc) across.

Row 13: Ch 5, turn; dc in next dc, (ch 2, dc in next dc) 12 times, place marker around last ch-2 made for st placement, (ch 2, dc in next dc) across.

Rows 14-25: Ch 5, turn; dc in next dc, (ch 2, dc in next dc) across.

Finish off.

RUFFLES
CENTER

With **right** side facing and working in ch-2 sps or around posts of dc as indicated by dots and arrows on Diagram, join Variegated with sc in marked ch-2 sp at Point A on Row 13 *(see Joining With Sc, page 1)*; 3 sc in same sp, (4 sc around dc or in ch-2 sp) around; join with slip st to first sc, finish off.

DIAGRAM

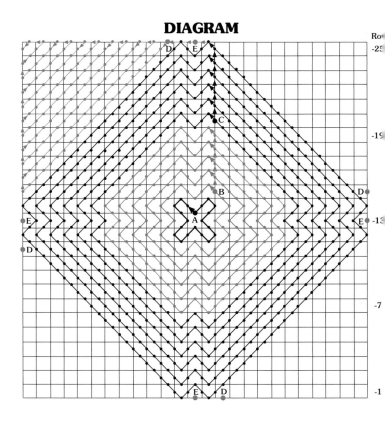

DIAMOND

Rnd 1: With **right** side facing and working in ch-2 sps or around posts of dc as indicated by dots and arrows on Diagram, page 5, join Green with slip st around dc at Point B on Row 15; ch 3, 3 dc around same dc, (4 dc in ch-2 sp or around dc) around; join with slip st to top of beginning ch-3.

Rnds 2-5: Slip st in next 3 dc, 4 dc around dc on next row, (4 dc in ch-2 sp or around dc) around; join with slip st to first dc.

Finish off.

OUTER

Rnd 1: With **right** side facing and working in ch-2 sps or around posts of dc as indicated by dots and arrows on Diagram, join Variegated with sc around dc at Point C on Row 20; 3 sc around same dc, (4 sc in ch-2 sp or around dc) around; join with slip st to first sc.

Rnds 2-6: Slip st in next 3 sc, 4 sc around dc on next row, (4 sc in ch-2 sp or around dc) around; join with slip st to first sc; at end of Rnd 6, do **not** finish off.

FIRST CORNER

Row 1: Slip st in next 7 sc, 4 sc in next sp (at Point E), slip st in next 4 sc, 4 sc in next sp (at Point D); working in ch-2 sps or around posts of dc as indicated by dots and arrows on Diagram, (4 sc in ch-2 sp or around dc) across, slip st in first sc of next 4-sc group.

Rows 2-11: Turn; slip st in last 4 sc made at end of previous row, working in ch-2 sps or around posts of dc as indicated by dots and arrows on Diagram, (4 sc in ch-2 sp or around dc) across, slip st in first sc of next 4-sc group.

Finish off.

SECOND CORNER

Row 1: With **right** side facing, join Variegated with sc in sp between 2 Outer Ruffles (at Point E); 3 sc in same sp, slip st in next 4 sc, 4 sc in next sp (at Point D); working in ch-2 sps or around posts of dc as indicated by dots and arrows on Diagram, (4 sc in ch-2 sp or around dc) across, slip st in first sc of next 4-sc group.

Rows 2-11: Turn; slip st in last 4 sc made at end of previous row, working in ch-2 sps or around posts of dc as indicated by dots and arrows on Diagram, (4 sc in ch-2 sp or around dc) across, slip st in first sc of next 4-sc group.

Finish off.

Work remaining 2 corners in same manner.

4. ZIGZAG

Finished Size: 8$^1/_4$" square

MATERIALS

100% Cotton Worsted Weight Yarn:
   Green - 1 ounce, (30 grams, 55 yards)
   Off-White - $^3/_4$ ounce, (20 grams, 40 yards)
Crochet hook, size G (4.00 mm) **or** size needed
   for gauge
Yarn needle

GAUGE: Each Triangle = 5$^1/_2$" x 5$^1/_2$" x 7$^3/_4$"

STITCH GUIDE

> **BEGINNING BLOCK**
> Ch 6 **loosely**, turn; dc in fourth ch from hook and in next 2 chs.
>
> **BLOCK**
> Slip st in ch-3 sp of next Block, ch 3, 3 dc in same sp.

TRIANGLE (Make 4)

Row 1 (Right side)**:** With Off-White, ch 6, dc in fourth ch from hook and in next 2 chs **(first Block made)**.

Note: Loop a short piece of yarn around any stitch to mark Row 1 as **right** side.

Row 2: Work Beginning Block, slip st around beginning ch of previous Block **(Fig. A)**, ch 3, 3 dc in same sp **(Fig. B)** changing to Green in last dc made **(Fig. 4b, page 2)**: 2 Blocks.

Fig. A

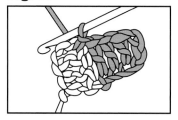

Fig. B

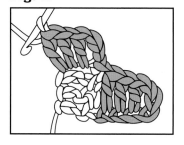

Continued on page 7.

Row 3: Work Beginning Block, slip st in ch-3 sp of first Block, ch 3, 3 dc in same sp, work Block: 3 Blocks.

Rows 4 and 5: Work Beginning Block, slip st in ch-3 sp of first Block, ch 3, 3 dc in same sp, work Blocks across changing to Off-White in last dc on Row 5: 5 Blocks.

Rows 6 and 7: Work Beginning Block, slip st in ch-3 sp of first Block, ch 3, 3 dc in same sp, work Blocks across changing to Green in last dc on Row 7: 7 Blocks.

Row 8: Ch 4, turn; sc in second ch from hook, dc in next 2 chs, (slip st, sc, 2 dc) in ch-3 sp of each Block across; finish off.

ASSEMBLY

With **right** sides facing, matching sts, and using corresponding colors, sew Triangles together to form one Square.

TRIM

With **right** side facing and working in Back Loops Only **(Fig. 1, page 2)**, join Green with slip st any st; slip st **loosely** in each st around; join with slip st to **both** loops of first slip st, finish off.

Design by Diana May.

5. SNOWFLAKE

Finished Size: 11"w x 9¼"h

MATERIALS
100% Cotton Worsted Weight Yarn;
   Blue - 1¼ ounces, (35 grams, 65 yards)
   Off-White - ¾ ounce, (20 grams, 40 yards)
Crochet hook, size G (4.00 mm) **or** size needed
   for gauge
Safety pin

GAUGE: In pattern, (3 dc, ch 1) 5 times = 4"

STITCH GUIDE

TREBLE CROCHET *(abbreviated tr)*
YO twice, insert hook in st indicated, YO and pull up a loop (4 loops on hook), (YO and draw through 2 loops on hook) 3 times.

CLUSTER (uses 2 dc and one sp)
YO twice, insert hook from **front** to **back** around post of first dc of last 3-dc group *(Fig. 3, page 2)*, YO and pull up a loop, (YO and draw through 2 loops on hook) twice (2 loops remaining on hook), YO twice, insert hook in ch-1 sp one row **below**, YO and pull up a loop, (YO and draw through 2 loops on hook) twice (3 loops remaining on hook), YO twice, insert hook from **front** to **back** around post of third dc of next 3-dc group, YO and pull up a loop, (YO and draw through 2 loops on hook) twice, YO and draw through all 4 loops on hook.

DISHCLOTH BODY

With Blue, ch 51, place marker in third ch from hook for st placement.

Row 1 (Right side)**:** Dc in fourth ch from hook **(3 skipped chs count as first dc)** and in next 2 chs, ch 1, ★ skip next ch, dc in next 3 chs, ch 1; repeat from ★ across to last 5 chs, skip next ch, dc in last 4 chs: 38 dc and 11 ch-1 sps.

Note: Loop a short piece of yarn around any stitch to mark Row 1 as **right** side.

Row 2: Ch 3 **(counts as first dc, now and throughout)**, turn; (dc in next 3 dc, ch 1) across to last 4 dc, dc in last 4 dc.

Row 3: Ch 3, turn; (dc in next 3 dc, ch 1) across to last 4 dc, dc in last 4 dc; place loop from hook onto safety pin to keep piece from unraveling as you work the next row.

Row 4: With **right** side facing, skip first dc and join Off-White with sc in sp **before** next dc *(see Joining With Sc, page 1)*; (ch 3, sc in next ch-1 sp) twice, work Cluster, sc in same sp as last sc made, ★ (ch 3, sc in next ch-1 sp) 4 times, work Cluster, sc in same sp as last sc made; repeat from ★ once **more**, ch 3, sc in last ch-1 sp, ch 3, skip next 3 dc, sc in sp **before** last dc; finish off.

Row 5: With **wrong** side facing, remove safety pin from Blue and place loop onto hook; ch 3, 3 dc in next ch-3 sp, (ch 1, 3 dc in next ch-3 sp) across, dc in last dc on Row 3; place loop from hook onto safety pin to keep piece from unraveling as you work the next row.

Row 6: With **right** side facing, skip first dc and join Off-White with sc in sp **before** next dc; ch 3, sc in next ch-1 sp, ★ † working in **front** of next 3-dc group, tr in next Cluster on Row 4, ch 3, sc in next ch-1 sp on Row 5, tr in same st as last tr made, sc in same sp on Row 5 as last sc made, ch 3, working in **front** of next 3-dc group, tr in same st as last tr made, sc in next ch-1 sp on Row 5 †, (ch 3, sc in next ch-1 sp) twice; repeat from ★ once **more**, then repeat from † to † once, ch 3, skip next 3 dc, sc in sp **before** last dc; finish off.

Row 7: With **right** side facing, remove safety pin from Blue and place loop onto hook; ch 3, 3 dc in next ch-3 sp, (ch 1, 3 dc in next ch-3 sp) across, dc in last dc on Row 5.

Rows 8 and 9: Ch 3, turn; (dc in next 3 dc, ch 1) across to last 4 dc, dc in last 4 dc; at end of Row 9, place loop from hook onto safety pin to keep piece from unraveling as you work the next row.

Row 10: With **right** side facing, skip first dc and join Off-White with sc in sp **before** next dc; ★ (ch 3, sc in next ch-1 sp) 4 times, work Cluster, sc in same sp as last sc made; repeat from ★ once **more**, ch 3, (sc in next ch-1 sp, ch 3) 3 times, skip next 3 dc, sc in sp **before** last dc; finish off.

Row 11: With **wrong** side facing, remove safety pin from Blue and place loop onto hook; ch 3, 3 dc in next ch-3 sp, (ch 1, 3 dc in next ch-3 sp) across, dc in last dc on Row 9; place loop from hook onto safety pin to keep piece from unraveling as you work the next row.

Row 12: With **right** side facing, skip first dc and join Off-White with sc in sp **before** next dc; (ch 3, sc in next ch-1 sp) 3 times, † working in **front** of next 3-dc group, tr in next Cluster on Row 10, ch 3, sc in next ch-1 sp on Row 11, tr in same st as last tr made, sc in same sp on Row 11 as last sc made, ch 3, working in **front** of next 3-dc group, tr in same st as last tr made, sc in next ch-1 sp on Row 11 †, (ch 3, sc in next ch-1 sp) twice, repeat from † to † once, ch 3, (sc in next ch-1 sp, ch 3) twice, skip next 3 dc, sc in sp **before** last dc; finish off.

Row 13: With **right** side facing, remove safety pin from Blue and place loop onto hook; ch 3, 3 dc in next ch-3 sp, (ch 1, 3 dc in next ch-3 sp) across, dc in last dc on Row 11.

Rows 14 and 15: Ch 3, turn; (dc in next 3 dc, ch 1) across to last 4 dc, dc in last 4 dc; at end of Row 15, place loop from hook onto safety pin to keep piece from unraveling as you work the next row.

Row 16: With **right** side facing, skip first dc and join Off-White with sc in sp **before** next dc; (ch 3, sc in next ch-1 sp) twice, work Cluster, sc in same sp as last sc made, ★ (ch 3, sc in next ch-1 sp) 4 times, work Cluster, sc in same sp as last sc made; repeat from ★ once **more**, ch 3, sc in last ch-1 sp, ch 3, skip next 3 dc, sc in sp **before** last dc; finish off.

Row 17: With **wrong** side facing, remove safety pin from Blue and place loop onto hook; ch 3, 3 dc in next ch-3 sp, (ch 1, 3 dc in next ch-3 sp) across, dc in last dc on Row 15; place loop from hook onto safety pin to keep piece from unraveling as you work the next row.

Row 18: With **right** side facing, skip first dc and join Off-White with sc in sp **before** next dc; ch 3, sc in next ch-1 sp, ★ † working in **front** of next 3-dc group, tr in next Cluster on Row 16, ch 3, sc in next ch-1 sp on Row 17, tr in same st as last tr made, sc in same sp on Row 17 as last sc made, ch 3, working in **front** of next 3-dc group, tr in same st as last tr made, sc in next ch-1 sp on Row 17 †, (ch 3, sc in next ch-1 sp) twice; repeat from ★ once **more**, then repeat from † to † once, ch 3, skip next 3 dc, sc in sp **before** last dc; finish off.

Row 19: With **right** side facing, remove safety pin from Blue and place loop onto hook; ch 3, 3 dc in next ch-3 sp, (ch 1, 3 dc in next ch-3 sp) across, dc in last dc on Row 17.

Rows 20 and 21: Ch 3, turn; (dc in next 3 dc, ch 1) across to last 4 dc, dc in last 4 dc.

Finish off.

EDGING

Rnd 1: With **right** side facing, join White with sc in first dc on Row 21; ch 3, sc in same st, ch 3, (sc in next ch-1 sp, ch 3) across to last 4 dc, skip next 3 dc, (sc, ch 3) twice in last dc; working in end of rows, sc in top of next dc row, ch 3) across; working in free loops *(Fig. 2b, page 2)* and in sps of beginning ch, (sc, ch 3) twice in first ch, (sc in next sp, ch 3) across, (sc, ch 3) twice in marked ch; working in end of rows, sc in top of same dc row, ch 3, (sc in top of next dc row, ch 3) across to last dc row, skip last dc row; join with slip st to first sc: 58 sc and 58 ch-3 sps.

Rnd 2: Slip st in first ch-3 sp, ch 1, (sc, ch 3) twice in same ch-3 sp and in each ch-3 sp around; join with slip st to first sc, finish off.

Design by Pat Gibbons.

6. HEXAGON

Finished Size: $11^1/2$" from point to point

MATERIALS
100% Cotton Worsted Weight Yarn:
Off-White - $1^1/4$ ounces, (35 grams, 65 yards)
Lavender - $^1/2$ ounce, (15 grams, 25 yards)
Crochet hook, size G (4.00 mm) **or** size needed
for gauge

GAUGE: Rnds 1-3 = $3^1/4$" diameter

STITCH GUIDE

> **BEGINNING SHELL**
> Ch 3, (dc, ch 2, 2 dc) in ch-2 sp indicated.
>
> **SHELL**
> (2 Dc, ch 2, 2 dc) in ch-2 sp indicated.
>
> **PICOT**
> Ch 3, slip st in top of last dc made.

DISHCLOTH
With Lavender, ch 7; join with slip st to form a ring.

Rnd 1 (Right side)**:** Ch 3 **(counts as first dc, now and throughout)**, 15 dc in ring; join with slip st to first dc: 16 dc.

Note: Loop a short piece of yarn around any stitch to mark Rnd 1 as **right** side.

Rnd 2: Ch 3, dc in same st and in next dc, (2 dc in next dc, dc in next dc) around; join with slip st to first dc: 24 dc.

Rnd 3: Ch 3, dc in next dc, ch 2, (dc in next 2 dc, ch 2) around; join with slip st to first dc, finish off: 12 ch-2 sps.

Rnd 4: With **right** side facing, join Off-White with slip st in any ch-2 sp; work Beginning Shell in same sp, (dc, ch 2, dc) in next ch-2 sp, ★ work Shell in next ch-2 sp, (dc, ch 2, dc) in next ch-2 sp; repeat from ★ around; join with slip st to first dc: 12 ch-2 sps.

Rnd 5: Slip st in next dc and in next ch-2 sp, work Beginning Shell in same sp, ch 4, sc in next ch-2 sp, ch 4, ★ work Shell in next ch-2 sp, ch 4, sc in next ch-2 sp, ch 4; repeat from ★ around; join with slip st to first dc: 18 sps.

Rnd 6: Slip st in next dc and in next ch-2 sp, work Beginning Shell in same sp, ch 3, (sc in next ch-4 sp, ch 3) twice, ★ work Shell in next ch-2 sp, ch 3, (sc in next ch-4 sp, ch 3) twice; repeat from ★ around; join with slip st to first dc: 24 sps.

Rnd 7: Slip st in next dc and in next ch-2 sp, work Beginning Shell in same sp, ch 3, (sc in next ch-3 sp, ch 3) 3 times, ★ work Shell in next ch-2 sp, ch 3, (sc in next ch-3 sp, ch 3) 3 times; repeat from ★ around; join with slip st to first dc: 30 sps.

Rnd 8: Slip st in next dc and in next ch-2 sp, ch 3, [dc, (ch 2, 2 dc) twice] in same sp, (ch 3, sc in next ch-3 sp) twice, sc in next sc, (sc in next ch-3 sp, ch 3) twice, ★ 2 dc in next ch-2 sp, (ch 2, 2 dc in same sp) twice, (ch 3, sc in next ch-3 sp) twice, sc in next sc, (sc in next ch-3 sp, ch 3) twice; repeat from ★ around; join with slip st to first dc: 30 sc and 36 sps.

Rnd 9: Slip st in next dc and in next ch-2 sp, work Beginning Shell in same sp, work Shell in next ch-2 sp, ★ † sc in next ch-3 sp, ch 3, sc in next ch-3 sp and in next 3 sc, sc in next ch-3 sp, ch 3, sc in next ch-3 sp †, work Shell in each of next 2 ch-2 sps; repeat from ★ 4 times **more**, then repeat from † to † once; join with slip st to first dc: 42 sc and 24 sps.

Rnd 10: Slip st in next dc and in next ch-2 sp, work Beginning Shell in same sp, ★ † ch 2, work Shell in next ch-2 sp, skip next 2 dc, sc in next sc, ch 3, skip next sc, sc in next 3 sc, ch 3, skip next sc, sc in next sc †, work Shell in next ch-2 sp; repeat from ★ 4 times **more**, then repeat from † to † once; join with slip st to first dc, finish off: 30 sc and 30 sps.

Rnd 11: With **right** side facing, join Lavender with slip st in first ch-2 sp; ch 3, (dc, work Picot, 2 dc) in same sp, ★ † [ch 2, (2 dc, work Picot, 2 dc) in next ch-2 sp] twice, ch 3, sc in next ch-3 sp, skip next sc, (dc, work Picot, dc) in next sc, sc in next ch-3 sp, ch 3 †, (2 dc, work Picot, 2 dc) in next ch-2 sp; repeat from ★ 4 times **more**, then repeat from † to † once; join with slip st to first dc, finish off.

Design by Gloria Graham.

7. WATERMELON MITT

Finished Size: 9³/₄" diameter

MATERIALS

100% Cotton Worsted Weight Yarn:
    Red - 2 ounces, (60 grams, 105 yards)
    Green - ¹/₂ ounce, (15 grams, 25 yards)
    Lt Green - 14 yards
    Black - small amount
Crochet hook, size G (4.00 mm) **or** size needed
    for gauge
Yarn needle

GAUGE: Rnds 1-3 = 3³/₄" diameter

WATERMELON (Make 2)

Rnd 1 (Right side): With Red, ch 4, 12 dc in fourth ch from hook **(3 skipped chs count as first dc)**; join with slip st to first dc: 13 dc.

Note: Loop a short piece of yarn around any stitch to mark Rnd 1 as **right** side.

Rnd 2: Ch 3 **(counts as first dc, now and throughout)**, dc in same st, 2 dc in each dc around; join with slip st to first dc: 26 dc.

Rnd 3: Ch 3, 2 dc in next dc, (dc in next dc, 2 dc in next dc) around; join with slip st to first dc: 39 dc.

Rnd 4: Ch 3, dc in next dc, 2 dc in next dc, (dc in next 2 dc, 2 dc in next dc) around; join with slip st to first dc: 52 dc.

Rnd 5: Ch 3, (dc in next 4 dc, 2 dc in next dc) 5 times, dc in next 5 dc, 2 dc in next dc, (dc in next 4 dc, 2 dc in next dc) around; join with slip st to first dc: 62 dc.

Rnd 6: Ch 3, (dc in next 4 dc, 2 dc in next dc) twice, ★ (dc in next 5 dc, 2 dc in next dc) twice, dc in next 4 dc, 2 dc in next dc; repeat from ★ 2 times **more**; join with slip st to first dc: 73 dc.

Rnd 7: Ch 3, (dc in next 8 dc, 2 dc in next dc) around; join with slip st to first dc, finish off: 81 dc.

Rnd 8: With **right** side facing, join Lt Green with sc in any dc **(see Joining With Sc, page 1)**; (sc in next 12 dc, 2 sc in next dc) twice, ★ sc in next 13 dc, 2 sc in next dc, sc in next 12 dc, 2 sc in next dc; repeat from ★ once **more**; join with slip st to first sc, finish off: 87 sc.

Rnd 9: With **right** side facing, join Green with sc in any sc; (sc in next 13 sc, 2 sc in next sc) twice, ★ sc in next 14 sc, 2 sc in next sc, sc in next 13 sc, 2 sc in next sc; repeat from ★ once **more**; join with slip st to first sc, finish off: 93 sc.

SEEDS

With Black and using photo as a guide for placement, add lazy daisy stitch seeds **(Fig. 6, page 2)**.

EDGING

With **wrong** sides together and working through **both** loops on **both** pieces, join Green with sc in any sc; sc in next 72 sc; working in sts on facing Watermelon piece only, sc in last 20 sc; join with slip st to first sc, ch 1, **turn**; working in sts on opposite Watermelon piece, sc in last 20 sc; finish off.

Design by Joyce L. Rodriguez.

9

17

8

11

12

11

15

10

3

7

8. SUNFLOWER

Finished Size: $8\frac{1}{4}$" square

MATERIALS
100% Cotton Worsted Weight Yarn:
    White - 1 ounce, (30 grams, 55 yards)
    Green - 14 yards
    Yellow - 8 yards
    Black - 5 yards
  Crochet hook, size H (5.00 mm) **or** size needed
    for gauge

GAUGE: Rnds 1-6 = $3\frac{3}{4}$" diameter

STITCH GUIDE

BEGINNING DECREASE
Pull up a loop in first 2 sc, YO and draw through all 3 loops on hook **(counts as one sc).**

ENDING DECREASE
Pull up a loop in last 2 sc, YO and draw through all 3 loops on hook **(counts as one sc).**

DISHCLOTH
CENTER
Do **not** join at end of Rnds 1-3. Place marker before first stitch of each round, moving marker after each round is complete.

Rnd 1 (Right side)**:** With Black, ch 2, 6 sc in second ch from hook; do **not** join.

Note: Loop a short piece of yarn around any stitch to mark Rnd 1 as **right** side.

Rnd 2: (2 Sc in next sc, sc in next 2 sc) twice: 8 sc.

Rnd 3: (2 Sc in next sc, sc in next sc) 4 times: 12 sc.

Rnd 4: (2 Sc in next sc, sc in next 2 sc) 4 times; slip st in next sc, finish off: 16 sc.

Rnd 5: With **right** side facing, join Yellow with slip st in any sc; [ch 4, slip st in second ch from hook, sc in next ch, hdc in last ch **(Petal made)]**, ★ slip st in next sc, ch 4, slip st in second ch from hook, sc in next ch, hdc in last ch; repeat from ★ around; join with slip st to first slip st, finish off: 16 Petals.

Rnd 6: With **right** side facing and working in chs at tip of Petals, join White with slip st in any Petal; (ch 3, slip st in next Petal) 3 times, ch 4, ★ slip st in next Petal, (ch 3, slip st in next Petal) 3 times, ch 4; repeat from ★ 2 times **more**; join with slip st to first slip st, finish off: 16 sps.

Rnd 7: With **right** side facing, join Green with dc in any ch-4 sp *(see Joining With Dc, page 1)*; (2 dc, ch 3, 3 dc) in same sp, sc in next ch-3 sp, (ch 2, sc in next ch-3 sp) twice, ★ (3 dc, ch 3, 3 dc) in next ch-4 sp, sc in next ch-3 sp, (ch 2, sc in next ch-3 sp) twice; repeat from ★ 2 times **more**; join with slip st to first dc, finish off.

FIRST CORNER
Row 1: With **right** side facing, join White with sc in any corner ch-3 sp *(see Joining With Sc, page 1)*; sc in same sp and in each st and each sp across to next corner ch-3 sp, 2 sc in corner ch-3 sp, leave remaining sts and sps unworked: 15 sc.

Rows 2-7: Ch 1, turn; work beginning decrease, sc in each sc across to last 2 sc, work ending decrease: 3 sc.

Row 8: Ch 1, turn; pull up a loop in first 3 sc, YO and draw through all 4 loops on hook; finish off: one st.

SECOND AND THIRD CORNER
Row 1: With **right** side facing, join White with sc in same sp as last sc made on Row 1 of last Corner; sc in same sp and in each st and each sp across to next corner ch-3 sp, 2 sc in corner ch-3 sp, leave remaining sts and sps unworked: 15 sc.

Rows 2-8: Work same as First Corner.

LAST CORNER
Row 1: With **right** side facing, join White with sc in same sp as last sc made on Row 1 of Third Corner; sc in same sp and in each st and each sp across, 2 sc in same sp as first sc made on Row 1 of First Corner: 15 sc.

Rows 2-8: Work same as First Corner; at end of Row 8, do **not** finish off.

EDGING
Rnd 1: Ch 1, turn; 2 sc in first sc, sc in end of next 7 rows, hdc in next sp on Rnd 7 (between center 2 sc), sc in end of next 7 rows on next Corner, ★ 3 sc in next st on Row 8, sc in end of next 7 rows, hdc in next sp on Rnd 7 (between center 2 sc), sc in end of next 7 rows on next Corner; repeat from ★ 2 times **more**, sc in same st as first sc; join with slip st to first sc: 72 sts.

Rnd 2: Ch 6, do **not** turn; dc in same st, ★ dc in each st across to center sc of next corner 3-sc group, (dc, ch 3, dc) in center sc; repeat from ★ 2 times **more**, dc in each st across; join with slip st to third ch of beginning ch-6, finish off: 76 sts and 4 ch-3 sps.

Rnd 3: With **right** side facing, join Green with sc in any corner ch-3 sp; 2 sc in same sp, ★ sc in Back Loop Only of each st across to next corner ch-3 sp *(Fig. 1, page 2)*, 3 sc in corner ch-3 sp; repeat from ★ 2 times **more**, sc in Back Loop Only of each st across; join with slip st to **both** loops of first sc, finish off.

Design by Leana Moon.

13

9. STRAWBERRY MITT

Finished Size: 7"w x 7³/₄"h

MATERIALS

100% Cotton Worsted Weight Yarn:
Red - 1¹/₂ ounces, (40 grams, 80 yards)
Green - 8 yards
Black - small amount
Crochet hook, size H (5.00 mm) **or** size needed
for gauge
Yarn needle

GAUGE: 10 dc = 3"; Rows 1-7 = 3³/₄"h

BERRY (Make 2)

With Red, ch 9.

Row 1: Dc in third ch from hook and in each ch across: 7 dc.

Row 2 (Right side)**:** Ch 3 **(counts as first dc, now and throughout)**, turn; dc in same st and in next 5 dc, 2 dc in last dc: 9 dc.

Note: Loop a short piece of yarn around any stitch to mark Row 2 as **right** side.

Row 3: Ch 3, turn; dc in same st, 2 dc in next dc, dc in next 5 dc, 2 dc in each of last 2 dc: 13 dc.

Rows 4-8: Ch 3, turn; dc in same st and in each dc across to last dc, 2 dc in last dc: 23 dc.

Rows 9 and 10: Ch 3, turn; dc in next dc and in each dc across.

Rows 11 and 12: Ch 2 **(counts as first hdc)**, turn; hdc in next st, dc in next 19 dc, hdc in last 2 sts.

Row 13: Ch 1, turn; skip first hdc, hdc in next hdc, dc in next 7 dc, hdc in next 5 dc, dc in next 7 dc, hdc in next hdc, leave remaining hdc unworked: 21 sts.

Row 14: Ch 1, turn; sc in first hdc, hdc in next 7 dc, sc in next 2 hdc, slip st in next hdc, sc in next 2 hdc, hdc in next 7 dc, sc in next hdc; finish off.

LEAVES

With **right** side facing and working in sts across Row 14 of Berry, skip first 8 sts and join Green with sc in next sc *(see Joining With Sc, page 1)*; ★ ch 7, sc in second ch from hook and in next 5 chs, sc in next st on Berry; repeat from ★ 3 times **more**; finish off.

SEEDS

With Black and using photo as a guide for placement, make straight stitch V's randomly in Rows 6, 8, and 10 *(Fig. 5, page 2)*.

EDGING

Holding **wrong** side of Berries together, matching sts, and working in **both** loops on **both** pieces, skip next 6 hdc from Leaves (on Row 14) and join Red with slip st in next hdc; sc evenly around, ending in second st on Row 14, slip st in next hdc; finish off.

Design by Joyce L. Rodriguez.

10. CHECKERBOARD

Finished Size: 9"w x 9^1/$_4$"h

MATERIALS
100% Cotton Worsted Weight Yarn:
White - 1 ounce, (30 grams, 55 yards)
Red - ^{3}/$_4$ ounce, (20 grams, 40 yards)
Crochet hook, size G (4.00 mm) **or** size needed
for gauge

GAUGE: In pattern, (sc, ch 1) 5 times = 2^1/$_4$"

FOUNDATION BLOCK

With White, ch 12.

Row 1 (Right side)**:** Sc in second ch from hook, place marker around sc just made for st placement, ★ ch 1, skip next ch, sc in next ch; repeat from ★ across: 6 sc and 5 ch-1 sps.

Note: Loop a short piece of yarn around any stitch to mark Row 1 as **right** side.

Rows 2-11: Ch 1, turn; sc in first sc, ★ ch 1, skip next ch, sc in next sc; repeat from ★ across; at end of Row 11, finish off.

CHART

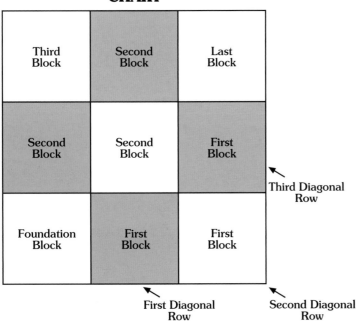

Third Block	Second Block	Last Block
Second Block	Second Block	First Block
Foundation Block	First Block	First Block

Third Diagonal Row

First Diagonal Row

Second Diagonal Row

FIRST DIAGONAL ROW
FIRST BLOCK

With **right** side facing, join Red with slip st in ch at base of marked sc on Row 1 of Foundation Block; ch 12.

Row 1 (Right side)**:** Sc in second ch from hook, place marker around sc just made for st placement, ★ ch 1, skip next ch, sc in next ch; repeat from ★ across; join with slip st to first sc on Row 1 of adjacent Block: 6 sc and 5 ch-1 sps.

Row 2: Ch 1, turn; sc in first sc, ★ ch 1, skip next ch, sc in next sc; repeat from ★ across.

Row 3: Ch 1, turn; sc in first sc, ★ ch 1, skip next ch, sc in next sc; repeat from ★ across; join with slip st to first sc on corresponding row of adjacent Block.

Rows 4-11: Repeat Rows 2 and 3, 4 times; do **not** finish off.

SECOND BLOCK

Row 1: Ch 1, do **not** turn; working in sts on Row 11 of Foundation Block, sc in first sc, ★ ch 1, skip next ch, sc in next sc; repeat from ★ across.

Rows 2-11: Ch 1, turn; sc in first sc, ★ ch 1, skip next ch, sc in next sc; repeat from ★ across; at end of Row 11, finish off.

SECOND DIAGONAL ROW
FIRST BLOCK

With **right** side facing, join White with slip st in ch at base of marked sc on Row 1 of First Block in First Diagonal Row; ch 12.

Row 1 (Right side)**:** Sc in second ch from hook, ★ ch 1, skip next ch, sc in next ch; repeat from ★ across; join with slip st to first sc on Row 1 of adjacent Block: 6 sc and 5 ch-1 sps.

Rows 2-11: Work same as First Block in First Diagonal Row.

SECOND BLOCK

Row 1: Ch 1, do **not** turn; working in sts on Row 11 of First Block in First Diagonal Row, sc in first sc, ★ ch 1, skip next ch, sc in next sc; repeat from ★ across; join with slip st to first sc on Row 1 of adjacent Block.

Rows 2-11: Work same as First Block in First Diagonal Row.

THIRD BLOCK

Row 1: Ch 1, do **not** turn; working in sts on Row 11 of Second Block in First Diagonal Row, sc in first sc, ★ ch 1, skip next ch, sc in next sc; repeat from ★ across.

Rows 2-11: Ch 1, turn; sc in first sc, ★ ch 1, skip next ch, sc in next sc; repeat from ★ across; at end of Row 11, finish off.

THIRD DIAGONAL ROW
FIRST BLOCK
Row 1: With **right** side facing, join Red with sc in first sc on Row 11 of First Block in Second Diagonal Row *(see Joining With Sc, page 1)*; ★ ch 1, skip next ch, sc in next sc; repeat from ★ across; join with slip st to first sc on Row 1 of adjacent Block.

Rows 2-11: Work same as First Block in First Diagonal Row.

SECOND BLOCK
Row 1: Ch 1, do **not** turn; working in sts on Row 11 of Second Block in Second Diagonal Row, sc in first sc, ★ ch 1, skip next ch, sc in next sc; repeat from ★ across; join with slip st to first sc on Row 1 of adjacent Block.

Row 2: Ch 1, turn; sc in first sc, ★ ch 1, skip next ch, sc in next sc; repeat from ★ across.

Row 3: Ch 1, turn; sc in first sc, ★ ch 1, skip next ch, sc in next sc; repeat from ★ across; join with slip st to first sc on corresponding row of adjacent Block.

Rows 4-11: Repeat Rows 2 and 3, 4 times; at end of Row 11, finish off.

LAST BLOCK
Row 1: With **right** side facing, join White with sc in first sc on Row 11 of First Block in Third Diagonal Row; ★ ch 1, skip next ch, sc in next sc; repeat from ★ across; join with slip st to first sc on Row 1 of adjacent Block.

Rows 2-11: Work same as Second Block in Third Diagonal Row.

EDGING
Rnd 1: With **right** side facing, join White with sc in first sc on Row 11 of Last Block; ch 1, sc in same st, ch 1, skip next ch, (sc in next sc, ch 1, skip next ch) 4 times, ★ (sc in next sc, ch 1) twice, skip next ch, (sc in next sc, ch 1, skip next ch) 4 times; repeat from ★ once **more**, (sc, ch 1) twice in last sc; working in end of rows, skip first row, (sc in next row, ch 1, skip next row) across; working in free loops of beginning ch *(Fig. 2b, page 2)*, (sc, ch 1) twice in first ch, skip next ch, (sc in next ch, ch 1, skip next ch) 4 times, **[**(sc in next ch, ch 1) twice, skip next ch, (sc in next ch, ch 1, skip next ch) 4 times**]** twice, (sc, ch 1) twice in next ch; working in end of rows, skip first row, (sc in next row, ch 1, skip next row) across; join with slip st to first sc: 72 ch-1 sps.

Rnd 2: Ch 1, sc in same st, ch 3, skip next sc, ★ sc in next sc, ch 3, skip next sc; repeat from ★ around; join with slip st to first sc, finish off.

Rnd 3: With **right** side facing and working **around** ch-3 on Rnd 2, join Red with slip st in any unworked sc on Rnd 1; ch 3, ★ drop loop from hook, insert hook from **front** to **back** in next unworked sc on Rnd 1, hook dropped loop and draw through, ch 3; repeat from ★ around; join with slip st to first slip st, finish off.

Design by Sarah Anne Phillips.

11. DIAGONAL RIDGES

Finished Size: 8¹/₂" square

MATERIALS
100% Cotton Worsted Weight Yarn:
1¹/₂ ounces, (40 grams, 80 yards)
Crochet hook, size G (4.00 mm) **or** size needed for gauge

GAUGE: Rows 1-8 = 3¹/₄" x 3¹/₄" x 4³/₄"

DISHCLOTH
Row 1: Ch 4, sc in second ch from hook and in next 2 chs: 3 sc.

Work in Back Loops Only throughout *(Fig. 1, page 2)*.

Row 2: Ch 1, turn; 2 sc in first sc, sc in next sc, 2 sc in last sc: 5 sc.

Rows 3-22: Ch 1, turn; 2 sc in first sc, sc in each sc across to last sc, 2 sc in last sc: 45 sc.

Rows 23-43: Ch 1, turn; pull up a loop in first 2 sts, YO and draw through all 3 loops on hook, sc in each sc across to last 2 sts, pull up a loop in last 2 sts, YO and draw through all 3 loops on hook: 3 sts.

Row 44: Ch 1, turn; pull up a loop in first 3 sts, YO and draw through all 4 loops on hook; finish off.

Design by Barbara Clark.

12. LITTLE FLOWERS

Finished Size: 9¹/₂"w x 9"h

MATERIALS
100% Cotton Worsted Weight Yarn:
  White - 1 ounce, (30 grams, 55 yards)
  Green - ³/₄ ounce, (20 grams, 40 yards)
  Yellow - 14 yards
Crochet hook, size G (4.00 mm) **or** size needed
  for gauge

GAUGE: 15 dc = 4"

STITCH GUIDE

> **SPLIT DOUBLE CROCHET**
> *(abbreviated Split dc)*
> YO, insert hook in same st as last Split dc made, YO
> and pull up a loop, YO and draw through 2 loops on
> hook, YO, skip next st or ch, insert hook in next st,
> YO and pull up a loop, YO and draw through
> 2 loops on hook, YO and draw through all 3 loops
> on hook.

DISHCLOTH BODY

With Green, ch 37, place marker in third ch from hook
for st placement.

Row 1 (Right side)**:** Dc in fourth ch from hook
(3 skipped chs count as first dc) and in each ch
across; finish off: 35 dc.

Note: Loop a short piece of yarn around any stitch to
mark Row 1 as **right** side.

Row 2: With **wrong** side facing, join Yellow with slip st
in first dc; (dc in next dc, slip st in next dc) across;
finish off.

Row 3: With **right** side facing, join White with dc in
first slip st *(see Joining With Dc, page 1)*; dc in each
st across; finish off.

Row 4: With **wrong** side facing, join Green with slip st
in first dc; (dc in next dc, slip st in next dc) across;
finish off.

Row 5: With **right** side facing, join White with dc in
first slip st; dc in each st across; finish off.

Row 6: With **wrong** side facing, join Yellow with slip st
in first dc; (dc in next dc, slip st in next dc) across;
finish off.

Row 7: With **right** side facing, join Green with dc in
first slip st; dc in each st across; finish off.

Row 8: With **wrong** side facing, join White with slip st
in first dc; (dc in next dc, slip st in next dc) across; do **not**
finish off.

Row 9: Ch 3 **(counts as first dc, now and
throughout)**, **turn**; dc in next dc and in each st across.

Row 10: Ch 3, turn; **[**YO, insert hook in first dc, YO
and pull up a loop, YO and draw through 2 loops on
hook, YO, skip next dc, insert hook in next dc, YO and
pull up a loop, YO and draw through 2 loops on hook,
YO and draw through all 3 loops on hook **(beginning
Split dc made)]**, (ch 1, work Split dc) across, dc in
same dc as last leg of last Split dc made.

Row 11: Ch 4 **(counts as first dc plus ch 1)**, turn;
[YO, insert hook in next st, YO and pull up a loop, YO
and draw through 2 loops on hook, YO, skip next ch,
insert hook in next st, YO and pull up a loop, YO and
draw through 2 loops on hook, YO and draw through all
3 loops on hook **(beginning Split dc made)]**, ch 1,
(work Split dc, ch 1) across to last dc, dc in last dc.

Row 12: Ch 3, turn; **[**YO, insert hook in first dc, YO
and pull up a loop, YO and draw through 2 loops on
hook, YO, skip next ch, insert hook in next st, YO and
pull up a loop, YO and draw through 2 loops on hook,
YO and draw through all 3 loops on hook **(beginning
Split dc made)]**, (ch 1, work Split dc) across, dc in
same dc as last leg of last Split dc made.

Row 13: Ch 3, turn; dc in each st and in each ch
across: 35 dc.

Row 14: Ch 1, turn; slip st in first dc, (dc in next dc,
slip st in next dc) across; finish off.

Row 15: With **right** side facing, join Green with dc in
first slip st; dc in each st across; finish off.

Rows 16-21: Repeat Rows 2-7; at end of Row 21, do
not finish off.

EDGING

(Slip st, ch 1) evenly across end of rows; working in free
loops of beginning ch *(Fig. 2b, page 2)*, slip st in first
ch, ch 1, (slip st in next ch, ch 1) across to marked ch,
slip st in marked ch, ch 1; (slip st, ch 1) evenly across
end of rows; working in sts on Row 21, slip st in first dc,
ch 1, (slip st in next dc, ch 1) across; join with slip st to
first slip st, finish off.

Design by Ruthie Marks.

17

13. WATERFALL

Finished Size: $9\frac{1}{2}$"w x $8\frac{3}{4}$"h

MATERIALS
100% Cotton Worsted Weight Yarn:
   Variegated - $1\frac{1}{2}$ ounces, (40 grams, 70 yards)
   Blue - $\frac{3}{4}$ ounce, (20 grams, 40 yards)
Crochet hook, size G (4.00 mm) **or** size needed
   for gauge

GAUGE: In pattern, 10 sts = 3"

STITCH GUIDE

FRONT POST DOUBLE CROCHET
(abbreviated FPdc)
YO, insert hook from **front** to **back** around post of dc indicated *(Fig. 3, page 2)*, YO and pull up a loop (3 loops on hook), (YO and draw through 2 loops on hook) twice.

FRONT POST TREBLE CROCHET
(abbreviated FPtr)
YO twice, insert hook from **front** to **back** around post of dc indicated *(Fig. 3, page 2)*, YO and pull up a loop (4 loops on hook), (YO and draw through 2 loops on hook) 3 times.

FRONT POST DOUBLE TREBLE CROCHET
(abbreviated FPdtr)
YO 3 times, insert hook from **front** to **back** around post of dc indicated *(Fig. 3, page 2)*, YO and pull up a loop (5 loops on hook), (YO and draw through 2 loops on hook) 4 times.

PICOT
Ch 2, sc in second ch from hook.

DISHCLOTH BODY
With Variegated, ch 33.

Row 1 (Right side)**:** Dc in fourth ch from hook **(3 skipped chs count as first dc)** and in each ch across: 31 dc.

Note: Loop a short piece of yarn around any stitch to mark Row 1 as **right** side.

Rows 2 and 3: Ch 3 **(counts as first dc, now and throughout)**, turn; dc in next dc and in each dc across. Finish off.

Row 4: With **right** side facing, join Blue with dc in first dc *(see Joining With Dc, page 1)*; ★ work FPdc around next dc, work FPtr around next dc one row **below**, work FPdtr around next dc 2 rows **below**, work FPtr around next dc one row **below**, work FPdc around next dc, dc in next dc; repeat from ★ across.

Rows 5 and 6: Ch 3, turn; dc in next st and in each st across.

Finish off.

Row 7: With **right** side facing, join Variegated with dc in first dc; work FPtr around next dc one row **below**, work FPdc around next dc, dc in next dc, work FPdc around next dc, work FPtr around next dc one row **below**, ★ work FPdtr around next dc 2 rows **below**, work FPtr around next dc one row **below**, work FPdc around next dc, dc in next dc, work FPdc around next dc, work FPtr around next dc one row **below**; repeat from ★ across to last dc, dc in last dc.

Rows 8 and 9: Ch 3, turn; dc in next st and in each st across; at end of last row, finish off.

Rows 10-16: Repeat Rows 4-9 once, then repeat Row 4 once **more**.

Finish off.

EDGING
With **right** side facing, join Variegated with sc in first dc on Row 16 *(see Joining With Sc, page 1)*; work Picot, ★ skip next st, sc in next st, work Picot; repeat from ★ across; working in end of rows, skip first row, (sc in top of next row, work Picot) across; working in free loops of beginning ch *(Fig. 2b, page 2)*, sc in first ch, work Picot, (skip next ch, sc in next ch, work Picot) 15 times; working in end of rows, sc in top of first row, work Picot, (sc in top of next row, work Picot) across to last row, skip last row; join with slip st to first sc, finish off.

Design by Joan E. Reeves.

14. DIAMOND OVERLAY

Finished Size: 8¼"w x 8"h

MATERIALS
100% Cotton Worsted Weight Yarn:
  1½ ounces, (40 grams, 80 yards)
Crochet hook, size G (4.00 mm) **or** size needed
  for gauge

GAUGE: In pattern, 11 sts = 3"

STITCH GUIDE

SPLIT CLUSTER (uses 3 sts)
Arm: YO, insert hook in Back Loop Only of dc indicated *(Fig. 1, page 2)*, YO and pull up a loop, YO and draw through 2 loops on hook (2 loops remaining on hook).

First Leg: YO twice, working in **front** of last row, insert hook in free loop of st indicated *(Fig. 2a, page 2)*, YO and pull up a loop (5 loops on hook), (YO and draw through 2 loops on hook) 3 times (2 loops remaining on hook).

Second Leg: YO twice, insert hook in free loop of st indicated, YO and pull up a loop (5 loops on hook), (YO and draw through 2 loops on hook) 4 times.

HALF CLUSTER (uses 2 sts)
Arm: YO, insert hook in Back Loop Only of dc indicated *(Fig. 1, page 2)*, YO and pull up a loop, YO and draw through 2 loops on hook (2 loops remaining on hook).

Leg: YO twice, working in **front** of last row, insert hook in free loop of st indicated *(Fig. 2a, page 2)*, YO and pull up a loop (5 loops on hook), (YO and draw through 2 loops on hook) 4 times.

DISHCLOTH BODY

Ch 29, place marker in third ch from hook for st placement.

Row 1 (Right side)**:** Dc in fourth ch from hook **(3 skipped chs count as first dc)** and in each ch across: 27 dc.

Row 2: Ch 3 **(counts as first dc, now and throughout)**, turn; dc in Front Loop Only of next dc and each dc across *(Fig. 1, page 2)*.

Row 3: Ch 3, turn; dc in Back Loop Only of next 3 dc, work Arm of Split Cluster in next dc, skip first dc on Row 1, work First Leg of Split Cluster in next dc, skip next 5 dc, work Second Leg of Split Cluster in next dc, ★ dc in Back Loop Only of next 5 dc on Row 2, work Arm of Split Cluster in next dc, work First Leg of Split Cluster in same st on Row 1 as Second Leg of last Split Cluster made, skip next 5 dc, work Second Leg of Split Cluster in next dc; repeat from ★ 2 times **more**, dc in Back Loop Only of last 4 dc on Row 2.

Row 4: Ch 3, turn; dc in Front Loop Only of next dc and each st across.

Row 5: Ch 3, turn; work Arm of Half Cluster in next dc, skip first 4 dc one row **below**, work Leg of Half Cluster in next Split Cluster, dc in Back Loop Only of next 5 dc on previous row, ★ work Arm of Split Cluster in next dc, work First Leg of Split Cluster in same st one row **below** as last Cluster made, skip next 5 dc, work Second Leg of Split Cluster in next Split Cluster, dc in Back Loop Only of next 5 dc on previous row; repeat from ★ 2 times **more**, work Arm of Half Cluster in next dc, work Leg of Half Cluster in same st one row **below** as Second Leg of last Split Cluster made, dc in Back Loop Only of last dc on previous row.

Row 6: Ch 3, turn; dc in Front Loop Only of next st and each st across.

Row 7: Ch 3, turn; dc in Back Loop Only of next 3 dc, work Arm of Split Cluster in next dc, skip first dc one row **below**, work First Leg of Split Cluster in next Half Cluster, skip next 5 dc, work Second Leg of Split Cluster in next Split Cluster, ★ dc in Back Loop Only of next 5 dc on previous row, work Arm of Split Cluster in next dc, work First Leg of Split Cluster in same st one row **below** as Second Leg of last Split Cluster made, skip next 5 dc, work Second Leg of Split Cluster in next Cluster; repeat from ★ 2 times **more**, dc in Back Loop Only of last 4 dc on previous row.

Rows 8-12: Repeat Rows 4-7 once, then repeat Row 4 once **more**; at end of Row 12, do **not** finish off.

EDGING

Ch 1, turn; slip st **loosely** in both loops of each dc across, ch 1; dc evenly spaced across end of rows, ch 1; working in free loops of beginning ch *(Fig. 2b, page 2)*, slip st **loosely** in each ch across and in marked ch, ch 1; dc evenly across end of rows, ch 1; join with slip st to first slip st, finish off.

Design by Barbara Clark.

19

15. STRIPED

Finished Size: 10"w x 11"h

MATERIALS
100% Cotton Worsted Weight Yarn:
Red - 1¹/₂ ounces, (40 grams, 80 yards)
White - ³/₄ ounce, (20 grams, 40 yards)
Crochet hook, size G (4.00 mm) **or** size needed
for gauge

GAUGE: In pattern, 17 sts = 3"

DISHCLOTH BODY
With Red, ch 57.

Row 1: Sc in third ch from hook, ★ ch 1, skip next ch, sc in next ch; repeat from ★ across: 28 sc and 28 sps.

Work in Front Loops Only of chs through Row 36 *(Fig. 1, page 2)*.

Row 2 (Right side)**:** Ch 2, turn; skip first sc, sc in next ch, ★ ch 1, skip next sc, sc in next ch; repeat from ★ 26 times **more** changing to White in last sc made *(Fig. 4a, page 2)*.

Note: Loop a short piece of yarn around any stitch to mark Row 2 as **right** side.

Continue changing colors in same manner throughout.

Row 3: With White, ch 2, turn; skip first sc, sc in next ch, ★ ch 1, skip next sc, sc in next ch; repeat from ★ across.

Rows 4-6: With Red, ch 2, turn; skip first sc, sc in next ch, ★ ch 1, skip next sc, sc in next ch; repeat from ★ across.

Row 7: With White, ch 2, turn; skip first sc, sc in next ch, ★ ch 1, skip next sc, sc in next ch; repeat from ★ across.

Row 8: With Red, ch 2, turn; skip first sc, sc in next ch, ★ ch 1, skip next sc, sc in next ch; repeat from ★ across.

Row 9: With White, ch 2, turn; skip first sc, sc in next ch, ★ ch 1, skip next sc, sc in next ch; repeat from ★ across.

Rows 10-12: With Red, ch 2, turn; skip first sc, sc in next ch, ★ ch 1, skip next sc, sc in next ch; repeat from ★ across.

Rows 13-36: Repeat Rows 3-12 twice, then repeat Rows 3-6 once **more**.

Finish off.

EDGING
Rnd 1: With **right** side facing, join White with sc in first ch-2 sp on Row 36 *(see Joining With Sc, page 1)*; 2 sc in same sp, ch 1, skip next sc, (sc in next sc, ch 1) across to last sc, 3 sc in last sc, ch 1 loosely; working in end of rows, skip first row, sc in next row, ch 1 loosely, (skip next row, sc in next row, ch 1 loosely) across to last 2 rows, skip last 2 rows; working in sps and in free loops of beginning ch *(Fig. 2b, page 2)*, 3 sc in first ch-2 sp, ch 1, skip next 2 chs, (sc in ch at base of next sc, ch 1, skip next ch) across to ch at base of last sc, 3 sc in ch at base of last ch, ch 1; working in end of rows, skip first row, (sc in next row, ch 1, skip next row) across; join with slip st to first sc, finish off.

Rnd 2: With **right** side facing and working in Back Loops Only, join Red with sc in center sc of any corner 3-sc group; 2 sc in same st, ★ ch 1, skip next sc, (sc in next ch, ch 1, skip next sc) across to center sc of next corner 3-sc group, 3 sc in center sc; repeat from ★ 2 times **more**, ch 1, skip next sc, (sc in next ch, ch 1, skip next sc) across; join with slip st to first sc, finish off.

Design by Mary C. Abadir.

16. COUNTRY GARDEN

Finished Size: 11" diameter

MATERIALS
100% Cotton Worsted Weight Yarn:
Green - 1 ounce, (30 grams, 55 yards)
Variegated - $^3/_4$ ounce, (20 grams, 35 yards)
Yellow - $^1/_2$ ounce, (15 grams, 25 yards)
Crochet hook, size H (5.00 mm) **or** size needed
for gauge

GAUGE: Rnds 1 and 2 = $2^3/_4$"

STITCH GUIDE

> **TREBLE CROCHET** *(abbreviated tr)*
> YO twice, insert hook in sc indicated, YO and pull
> up a loop (4 loops on hook), (YO and draw through
> 2 loops on hook) 3 times.
>
> **CLUSTER** *(uses one st)*
> ★ YO, insert hook in st indicated, YO and pull up a
> loop, YO and draw through 2 loops on hook; repeat
> from ★ once **more**, YO and draw through all
> 3 loops on hook.
>
> **PICOT**
> Ch 2, sc in second ch from hook.

DISHCLOTH

Rnd 1 (Right side)**:** With Yellow, ch 5, (dc, ch 1) 7 times
in fifth ch from hook; join with slip st to fourth ch of
beginning ch-5: 8 sts and 8 ch-1 sps.

Note: Loop a short piece of yarn around any stitch to
mark Rnd 1 as **right** side.

Rnd 2: [Ch 2, dc in same st **(first Cluster made)]**,
ch 1, work Cluster in next ch, ch 1, ★ work Cluster in
next dc, ch 1, work Cluster in next ch, ch 1; repeat from
★ around; join with slip st to first dc, finish off:
16 Clusters and 16 ch-1 sps.

Rnd 3: With **right** side facing, join Green with dc in
any Cluster *(see Joining With Dc, page 1)*; ch 1, dc in
same st, skip next ch, ★ (dc, ch 1, dc) in next Cluster,
skip next ch; repeat from ★ around; join with slip st to
Back Loop Only of first dc *(Fig. 1, page 2)*: 32 dc and
16 chs.

Rnd 4: Ch 1, working in Back Loops Only, sc in same
st and in each ch and each dc around; join with slip st to
both loops of first sc, finish off: 48 sc.

Rnd 5: With **right** side facing and working in both
loops, join Variegated with sc in any sc *(see Joining
With Sc, page 1)*; sc in next 2 sc, 2 sc in next sc, (sc in
next 3 sc, 2 sc in next sc) around; join with slip st to first
sc: 60 sc.

Rnd 6: Ch 1, **turn**; sc in same st, tr in next sc, (sc in
next sc pushing tr to right side, tr in next sc) around; join
with slip st to first sc.

Rnd 7: Ch 3 **(counts as first dc, now and
throughout)**, do **not** turn; dc in next tr and in each st
around; join with slip st to first dc, finish off.

Rnd 8: With **right** side facing, join Green with sc in any
dc; sc in same st and in next dc, (2 sc in next dc, sc in
next dc) around; join with slip st to first sc: 90 sc.

Rnd 9: Ch 1, **turn**; sc in same st, tr in next sc, (sc in
next sc pushing tr to right side, tr in next sc) around; join
with slip st to first sc.

Rnd 10: Ch 3, do **not** turn; dc in next tr and in each st
around; join with slip st to Front Loop Only of first dc.

Rnd 11: Ch 1, turn; sc in Back Loop Only of same st
and each dc around; join with slip st to **both** loops of
first sc, finish off.

Rnd 12: With **right** side facing and working in both
loops, join Variegated with slip st in any sc; ch 2, hdc in
next sc, 2 hdc in next sc, (hdc in next 2 sc, 2 hdc in next
sc) around; join with slip st to top of beginning ch-2,
finish off: 120 sts.

Rnd 13: With **right** side facing, join Yellow with sc in
same st as joining; work Picot, sc in same st and in next
2 hdc, ★ (sc, work Picot, sc) in next hdc, sc in next
2 hdc; repeat from ★ around; join with slip st to first sc,
finish off.

Design by Patti Robbins.